PENGUIN HANDBOOKS

Weight Training

Dr. Frank Ryan, who holds a Ph.D.
in psychology, was for many years
the varsity coach at Yale University
in New Haven and is renowned for his
success in applying his techniques
for the physical and mental conditioning of athletes in all sports.

ALSO BY DR. FRANK RYAN

DR. FRANK RYAN

Weight Training

PENGUIN BOOKS

Penguin Books Ltd, Harmondsworth,
Middlesex, England
Penguin Books, 625 Madison Avenue,
New York, New York 10022, U.S.A.
Penguin Books Australia Ltd, Ringwood,
Victoria, Australia
Penguin Books Canada Limited, 2801 John Street,
Markham, Ontario, Canada L3R 1B4
Penguin Books (N.Z.) Ltd, 182–190 Wairau Road,
Auckland 10, New Zealand

First published in the United States of America
in The Viking Library of Sports Skills
by The Viking Press 1969
Published in Penguin Books 1978
Reprinted 1978, 1979

LIBRARY OF CONGRESS CATALOGING IN PUBLICATION DATA
Ryan, Frank.
Weight training.
1. Weight lifting. 2. Physical fitness.
I. Title.
GV546.R9 1978   796.4'1   78–1499
ISBN 0 14 046.339 9

Printed in the United States of America by
The Book Press, Brattleboro, Vermont
Set in Linotype Caledonia

All illustrations by courtesy of Ryan Films, Inc.
Copyright © Ryan Films, Inc., 1963

Preface

The goal of this book is to help you become a better athlete. We assume that you are eager to do your best in your event and hope that by now you are convinced that you must have a weight-training program to bring out your potential.

As you will see, weight training is a natural, unmysterious activity, though its results often seem miraculous. To get the most out of your weight-training program there are a number of things that you ought to know. You surely do not need to be an expert in physiology and anatomy, but you will progress better if you know something about your muscles and how they work. One can learn to drive a car without knowing anything about the engine, but good drivers usually know how a car works.

A number of basic weight-training exercises have been developed. You should get familiar with these exercises and the effects that they produce. You should be able to perform all of them easily and correctly. In this book the descriptions of the exercises can be brief and simple, since we have photo sequences to illustrate them.

The basic exercises form your repertory. From these exercises you will create the programs that you will follow at different times. We will be giving examples of how and why a program is put together.

When you join a club, go out for a school team, or go to college, very elaborate weight-training facilities and equipment will probably be available to you. That will be helpful and convenient, but don't wait. You can make a start on your weight-training program with simple, inexpensive equipment. At the beginning all you will need will be a light barbell set and two dumbbells. As soon as you can, get a strong bench.

As you get stronger, you will want to buy more plates. Also, as you begin to work with heavier weights, you ought to get a reliable squat rack.

It is good to lift with other athletes. There are a number of advantages to having training partners. You can share equipment, draw mutual inspiration, and act as safety spotters for each other. If you carry out a sensible weight-training program, the results are sure-fire. You are going to be a stronger person and a better athlete.

Contents

Weight Training

Why Weight Training?

As a candidate for an athletic team, you will want to do your best. You will want to use the best training methods available to bring out your potential. Your coach and other interested people are going to urge you to train with weights. You may have some resistance to the suggestion and take the position: "I practice my event faithfully, condition myself, and compete well and often. Isn't that enough?" The answer is NO! Surely faithful practice, good conditioning, and plenty of competition are needed, but it is now clear that weight training is essential.

We live in an age of startling athletic performances. Not only are we in the midst of a record explosion, but the average level of athletic performance has risen enormously. Experienced coaches are shocked by the frequency with which new world records are set. In many events the ability to equal the world-record mark of a generation ago would not justify entering an athlete in championship competition. What is even more surprising to the old coach is to see an athlete of clearly average ability exceed the marks of yesterday's gifted greats.

To be sure, there have been advances in equipment, techniques, and other training methods, but the widespread use of weight training has been the single biggest factor behind the record explosion. In many athletic activities *all* successful men are weight trainers. In others nearly all athletes have a weight-training background.

As we look back now, the astonishing thing is that weight training hasn't been with us longer. It makes so much sense. But, after all, it took us a long time to realize that the world is round. Not long ago it wasn't simply a matter of weight training not being recommended. It was actually forbidden by most coaches. Athletes were warned that they would become "muscle-bound."

This reluctance to accept weight training in athletics appears to have derived from the fact that a generation ago much of the weight training was carried out by men who were basically nonathletic. They tended to be naturally slow, stiff-jointed, and uncoordinated. However, many of them developed fine physiques and were pressed into service by coaches. Because they really were not very athletic, they still did not perform exceptionally well (though a lot better than if they had not lifted in the first place). Then a false inference was made. It was reasoned that the awkwardness and stiffness of these men and their poor performances were due to weight training. They were pronounced "muscle-bound." It was hard to know that these men were stiff-jointed before they began lifting.

Over the years a few gifted athletes experimented with weight training and obtained good results. But their training methods attracted very little attention. Some coaches thought that their success was achieved despite the weight training. The 1950s was the decade of the great weight-training explosion. More and more talented athletes turned to this method. Records began to topple in bewildering fashion, and by 1960 weight-trained athletes began to dominate the scene. That domination is now very thorough.

The history of weight training and the results produced make an overwhelming case for its use. Yet we should have been able to figure this out in advance and predict the great value of this training method. In sports we learn "form," or technique, and these words often seem to acquire a magic. Some techniques place a premium on accuracy alone, for example, shooting a foul in basketball. Others, such as pitching a baseball, require both accuracy and power. Still others—putting the shot is an example—call for enormous power and relatively little accuracy.

Most athletic events require a certain amount of power, and in these events form is simply the efficiency with which power is applied. If we say that an athlete has good form, we simply mean that his balance, position, movements, and so on, are such that he is able to use his power efficiently. But he must have the power, and that's where weight training comes in.

1. We live in an age of startling athletic performance, and weight training methods have played a major role.

1*a*

1*b*

1*c*

1*d*

Your Muscles

The body is a truly magnificent machine. And it has to be, because it has a lot of complicated things to do as it makes its way through this world. In general, it takes in messages, evaluates them, and makes some kind of response. To carry out these functions the body is remarkably specialized. Tissues do different things. For example, certain tissues are sensitive to light, and from this sensitivity we have vision. Other tissues are sensitive to chemicals, and we have a sense of smell. Still other tissues are sensitive to sound, taste, or pain.

We can say that our sensory tissues form our window on the world. They bring in the messages. Other parts of the body, the central nervous system, which includes the brain, have the job of making sense out of these messages. When action is called for, impulses are sent to the muscles.

The muscles are made of a specialized tissue with two basic functions—to contract when stimulated and to relax when the stimulation stops. Actually, that's all that they can do. It may not seem like much, but it works out well.

If we were to look inside a muscle with a microscope, we would see that it is made up of thousands of fibers (photo series 2). These fibers are connected to the brain by way of the nerves. Let's consider a single fiber. If it receives a nervous impulse from the brain, it contracts. It becomes shorter and thicker (photo series 3). If enough fibers are stimulated, the entire muscle contracts. The strength of the muscle contraction will depend upon the number of fibers that are contracting at a given time and the strengths of the individual fibers involved. As we shall see, in most normal activities many of the fibers are not stimulated and therefore fail to con-

6

tribute to the over-all movement. Also, many of the fibers that do react are not nearly as strong as they could be.

Now let's go a step further. Remember, all that muscle fibers can do is contract and relax, and this must produce effective movement. Consider arm movement. We can visualize the arm as two members in a hinge relationship. When the fibers in the biceps muscle contract and become shorter, the resulting action flexes the arm. If contraction takes place in the triceps muscle, the large muscle in the back of the upper arm, the arm will straighten.

The major point is a simple one. The muscles that produce locomotion or manipulation can be divided into two groups—the flexors, or pulling muscles (photo series 4 and 5), and the extensors, or pushing muscles. But whether flexion or extension is produced depends on the rigging, the setup of the hinge arrangement. Either way, the muscle-fiber action is the same—contraction.

When you chin yourself, flexion of the arm is the essential movement. When you do a push-up, extension of the arm is what becomes important. But extension, like flexion, still depends on the contraction of muscle fibers (photo series 6 and 7). The stronger each fiber contraction and the more fibers involved, the greater the power. Let's again consider a single muscle fiber. Under conditions of regular stimulation both the diameter of the fiber itself and the covering of the fiber increase in size (photo series 8). This happens because effortful contraction against resistance breaks down the fiber, and when it grows back the body overcompensates and the muscle grows larger. This increase in thickness makes the fiber capable of a stronger contraction. In normal activity many fibers loaf; they are seldom if ever stimulated and fail to grow stronger. One of the goals of weight training is to stimulate the fibers that are not otherwise used.

Unfortunately, you cannot do anything to increase the number of fibers that make up a muscle. That number is fixed. What you can do is increase the thickness of individual fibers.

To work and grow fibers need to have nourishment and to have waste products removed. To provide fuel for growth and to eliminate the waste products generated by work, a muscle fiber depends on a network of capillaries (photo 9). With a great deal of work over sustained periods the capillaries widen and apparently increase in number. Since the supply of fuel and the elimination of waste products then become more efficient, endurance is increased.

Very heavy lifting stimulates all or most of the muscle fibers. The fibers react to regular stimulation by becoming thicker and stronger. As a result, the entire muscle tends to grow larger and stronger.

A general principle is seen. If you are training for an event that requires great strength or explosive power, you will lift heavy weights relatively few times. If your event requires endurance rather than power, you will work with lighter weights but perform more repetitions (photo 10). Within certain limits your body has an astonishing ability to adjust to almost any physical task given to it. As the task gets tougher the body gets tougher. But you have to give your body a chance. A few factors are needed. These are time, spacing, and progression. By time we mean simply that the body cannot make radical changes overnight. It needs time to adjust. By spacing we mean that the exercises must be carried out at regular intervals. The body responds best to a schedule that includes regular exercise followed by periods of rest. By progression we mean that the "doses" must become gradually stronger. In this way the body gets used to the new task and goal. In weight training poundage is gradually increased as the body becomes ready to accept increases.

"Adjustment" is the key word. If given a reasonable chance, the body adjusts to what is has to do—but it goes no farther! If you lift a sixty-pound weight over your head several times at regular intervals and do so over a period of time, the body adjusts to this task. But it does not adjust to the task of exercising with a hundred-pound weight—only the sixty-pound weight. After all, that's all that you required it to do.

Nearly all athletic events supply good exercise. The event makes demands on the body, and the body gets stronger and more efficient to carry out the event. But it only adjusts as much as it has to—no more. The gains in strength become less and less as the body gets used to the event. Potential strength and potential performance cannot be realized unless something else is done. This is where weight training comes in.

Weight training has produced such spectacular results that the original attitude of distrust toward this method has turned to one approaching awe or even magical expectation. But weight training has no magic to offer. It simply offers a chance to work under *controlled* conditions. Let's take a look.

Suppose we return to our picture of the muscle fiber. If the fiber is stimulated, it grows stronger and ready for increased work. If not, it fails to grow. In fact, even a fiber that has grown thick and strong will get thin and weak again if stimulation is not continued.

8

The over-all situation is simple. If muscles are to become stronger, they must have exercise. But remember that your muscles won't become any stronger than they have to be to do what you require of them. In most normal activities many fibers will receive little or no stimulation. They just won't grow.

Without some form of exercise your muscles will become small and weak. There are many kinds of exercise, and all of them do some good. Certainly you can benefit from sit-ups, push-ups, chins, and so on. The football player who returns to college after a summer of heavy construction work looks stronger and is stronger. Now, if all forms of exercise are good, what is so special about weight training? Why has this method been of such enormous importance?

The unique and great value of weight training lies in the control and precision that it permits. The control lies in two important areas. First, we know that certain exercises emphasize the use of particular muscles. This permits you to select exercises that improve the muscles essential to the performance of your event. Contrast this, let's say, with heavy construction work. Certainly this kind of work will make you stronger, but the muscles that are emphasized will be a matter of chance. You will have little or no control over which muscles will get attention.

Second, and even more important, weight training affords precise control over the poundages you are lifting. Such control is essential to the whole notion of progressive resistance. Just as the term implies, it means nothing more than that the resistance offered by an exercise is increased regularly as time goes by. This is the basic idea of modern training methods. It goes back to our knowledge that the body will adjust and become stronger if the exercise program gradually becomes harder.

When you do chins and push-ups, the serverity of the exercise task is pretty much determined by your body weight. And, of course, the body weight tends to be constant. You can gradually increase the number of chins or push-ups that you do, but the actual resistance remains about the same. It is possible to hang weights from your body when you are chinning or in push-ups to change the angle of your body, but weight training affords a much simpler and more convenient control. In weight training you know exactly what poundages you are adding.

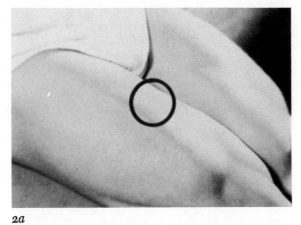

2a

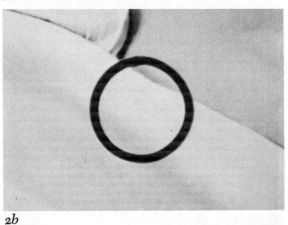

2b

2c

2. If we could look inside the muscle with a microscope, we would see that it is made up of thousands of fibers.

3. A muscle fiber contracts when it is stimulated.

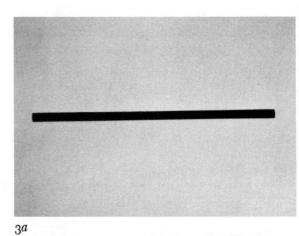

3a

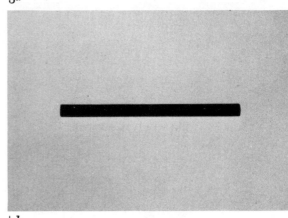

3b

3c

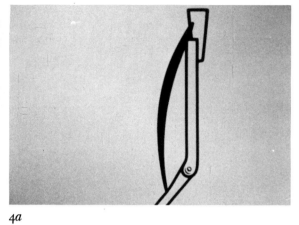

4a

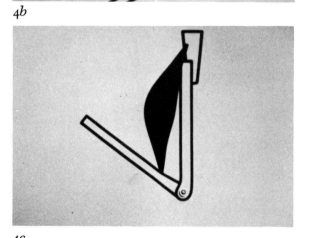

4b

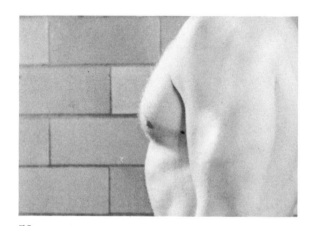

5. Compare man curling a weight with diagram (photo 4).

5a

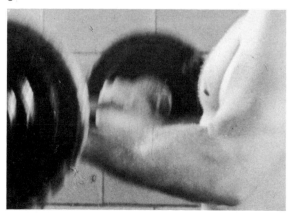

5b

4c

4. The muscle fibers contract to produce flexion of the arm.

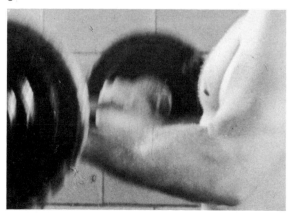

5c

6. Contraction of the muscle fibers can bring about extension.

7a

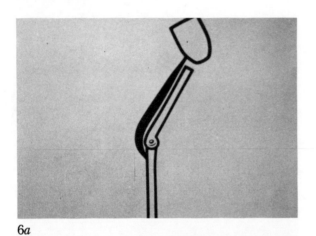

6a

7b

7. Compare the take-off action of the high jumper with the diagram. The more powerful the contraction the higher he will jump.

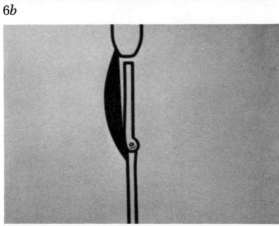

6b

6c

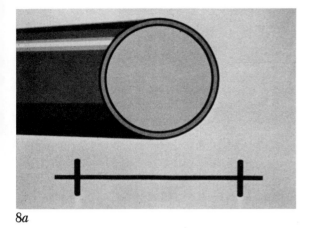

8*a*

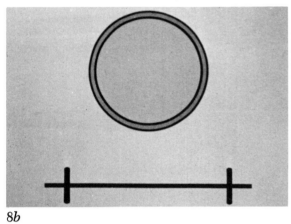

8*b*

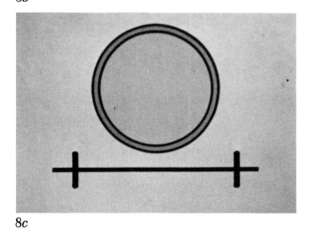

8*c*

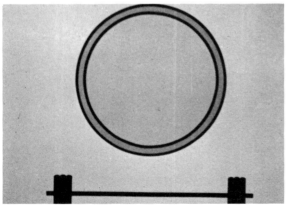

8*d*

8. If a muscle fiber is stimulated regularly both the diameter of the fiber itself and the covering of the fiber increase in size.

9. A network of capillaries supplies fuel to the fibers and eliminates their waste products.

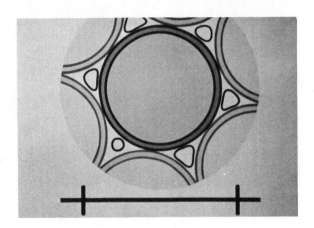

10. Summary of the effects produced by different conditions of work. Heavy work increases the size of the fibers. Sustained work makes for more efficient capillary action.

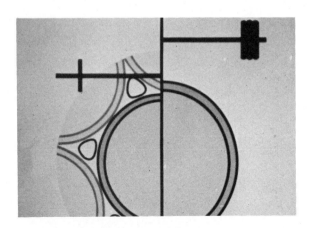

Weight Lifting

Just as men have always enjoyed competition in running, jumping, and throwing, it has always seemed natural for them to see who could lift the heaviest objects. Men of enormous physical strength became legends. Later on, the strongman became a popular fixture of the circus.

Out of man's fascination with strength weight lifting emerged as a sport in its own right. Competition is held throughout the nation and internationally, including the Olympic Games. There are standard rules that apply everywhere. As in boxing and wrestling, there are weight classes ranging from 123¼ pounds to unlimited, so that the size of the athlete is no obstacle to participation. Competition is held in three lifts, usually referred to as the Olympic lifts.

In this book we are not concerned directly with weight lifting as a sport. It has its own techniques and training methods, and a candidate for weight lifting must learn them. However, we will talk briefly about the Olympic lifts for two reasons. First, other sports owe much to competitive lifting. Second, the competitive lifts are valuable exercises.

Until recently the two-arms clean and press (photo series 11) was a popular competitive lift. Though this lift has been dropped from international competition, it remains a useful exercise. There are two parts to this lift. The first action is to clean, or lift, the weight to the chest. In making this movement use is made of the legs, trunk, and arms. The weight must then be held steadily in place until a signal is given by the referee. It is then pressed to arms' length overhead. This must be done without impetus from the legs or trunk. The two remaining lifts are as follows.

Two-arms snatch (photo series 12). In this, the second of the lifts, the weight must be raised overhead in a single, continuous movement. A pull of the legs and back starts the movement, and a smooth transfer of effort to the arms brings the weight overhead as the lifter lowers his body under the bar, either by squatting or by splitting his legs forward and back. He then completes the lift by standing erect.

Two-arms clean and jerk (photo series 13). Like the press the clean and jerk is a two-part lift. The legs, trunk, and arms pull the weight upward. The pull is continued until the legs are fully extended. Then the lifter lowers his body by either a split or a squat, catching the bar at his shoulders by whipping his elbows outward and up and turning his hands palms up. He then straightens his legs and assumes a comfortable erect position with the weight held at his shoulders. The jerk differs from the press in that powerful use is made of the legs in driving the weight overhead. At the height of their drive, the legs split to lower the body under the weight. An erect position is assumed with the weight overhead and under control.

It is obvious that fine weight lifters are extremely powerful men. They are, in fact, the strongest of all men. But more than sheer strength is needed. The three international lifts are truly athletic events with a premium on coordination, agility, balance, and speed. Any athlete will profit from trying to master the three standard lifts. The competitive lifts involve all of the muscles of the body and are therefore excellent exercises. They also afford basic training in the features needed for performance in almost all athletic events.

Warm-up. It is a curious fact of athletic life that the warm-up is usually slighted, neglected, or ignored. The average athlete has a tendency to regard his warm-up as an unimportant preliminary to be gotten out of the way quickly. Even the athlete who is willing to work hard at his event tends to forget his warm-up. Of course, this is not true of the experienced athlete, because he has become firmly convinced of the great importance of a thorough warm-up.

A good warm-up (photo series 14) causes the muscles to become saturated with blood, leaving them looser and ready for work. Both soreness and the chances of injury are reduced. The content of the warm-up can be selected from a great variety of exercises, but running should be included. The main point is that there should be enough of it. Also, on your weight-training days the first lifts should be done easily and with light weights.

The coach is forced to spend a lot of his time and energy in reminding and urging the average candidate to warm up properly. Surprise him by already having good warm-up habits.

Basic Exercises. The use of barbells, dumbbells, benches, iron boots, and other pieces of apparatus makes possible a great variety of exercises. This section describes the so-called basic exercises. These are the exercises that the great athletes have found to be the most helpful.

Remember that muscles do not work in isolation. The basic exercises always involve many muscles. However, most of the exercises emphasize the use of specific muscles. You can develop the muscles that are most important to your event by selecting the exercises that put an emphasis on these muscles.

As you read the descriptions and particularly as you look at the picture sequences, the movements of each exercise will start to become clear. Work with very light weights while you are getting the feel of the exercises. In some instances it might be best to work with the bar alone.

Compared with the various sports, weight training is a relatively safe activity, and, of course, you will want to keep it that way for you. So from the very beginning establish safe lifting habits. Be sure that you learn to carry out every exercise correctly.

Press (photo series 15). This exercise is closely related to the first of the competitive lifts. It differs from the competitive version of the press only in that the lifter does not use back-bend to aid him in getting the weight overhead. The head is drawn slightly back to permit the bar to pass. Eyes are level.

The phrase "to clean" simply means to bring the barbell up to position for the press (photo series 16). The lifter prepares for the clean by standing very close to the bar. He then lowers his hips, keeping his back straight and his head erect. A straight back is important in reducing strain. In the normal press the hands are spaced about shoulder width. A drive of the legs and a pull of the arm start the upward movement of the weight.

The average athlete does not pay enough attention to the clean. There is a tendency to haul or wrestle the barbell to the chest. Efficient technique for the clean is easy to understand. It is just a matter of making the right way a habit. Keep these three main points in mind: (1) stand close to the bar, (2) keep a straight back, and (3) drive with the legs to start the weight moving.

The press works the triceps muscles, which are located in the back of the upper arm (photo 17). The action of the triceps is to straighten the arm.

The *curl* (photo series 18) is a widely used and important exercise for the development of the biceps and forearms. It can be said to be the complement of the press. The press emphasizes the extensor muscles of the arm; the curl uses the flexors.

In the normal curl the bar is grasped with the palms up. The hands are spaced so as to keep the elbows close to the body. The barbell is raised from a position across the thighs to a position at the base of the neck. The elbows remain close to the body during the exercise. Ideally, the barbell is raised only by flexing the arms. The trunk and legs are kept straight.

The *bench press* (photo series 19), a fine developer of the triceps, shoulders, and chest, is one of the most valuable of all exercises. It seems to find its way into the programs of nearly all athletes. Pressing is carried out while lying supine on a strong and reliable bench. The weight is pushed from the chest to an upward position in which the arms are straight.

The spacing of the hands on the bar can be varied to place emphasis on either the arms or the chest muscles. With a narrow grip the triceps are chiefly involved. If the grip is made very wide, the pectoral muscles of the chest came strongly into play. The main function of these muscles is to rotate the arms inward. Hence, as the grip is widened, contraction of the pectorals is increasingly emphasized in raising the barbell.

As you progress in your training, you will be able to bench press fairly heavy weights. Thus, at an advanced state, it is best to have training partners standing by to help place and remove the weight.

The *dumbbell raises* are shoulder exercises. The deltoid muscle covers the shoulder. Its function is to elevate the arms. As you can see in the photos (series 20), the deltoid is divided into three parts. To develop all parts of the deltoid muscle dumbbell raises are carried out in a number of ways. With the athlete standing, the dumbbells can be raised sideways to a position directly overhead (photo series 21). This exercise is started with the palms toward the thighs. To complete the raise to the overhead position rotate your hands, but delay this rotation as long as possible.

From an erect position the dumbbells can be brought forward and upward. This exercise can be done with alternating movements of the arms (photo series 22) or with both arms raised together (photo series 23).

Lateral raises can be performed from a bent-over position (photo series 24). From this position the dumbbells are raised to the point where the arms become parallel to the ground or slightly higher. From this same bent-over position it is also possible to carry out backward raises.

In all of the dumbbell raises the trunk and legs remain steady and should not contribute to the raising of the dumbbells. Also, emphasis on deltoid action is greatest when the arms are kept straight. Nevertheless, a slight bend of the arms is desirable because it takes strain off the elbows.

18

The *straight arm pull-over* (photo series 25) affects the chest muscles, and when carried out with heavy breathing tends to increase the size of the rib cage (photo series 26). With the athlete lying supine on the bench the weight is pushed up from the chest until the arms are straight. It is then lowered back over the head to a point about level with the bench. Inhale fully as you lower the weight and exhale as you lift it back.

Because of the unfavorable leverage position that this exercise affords only very light weights are used. For beginning lifters it is best to start with only the weight of the bar.

Lateral raises lying (photo series 27 and 28), or "flying exercises" as they are commonly called, are direct developers of the pectoral or chest muscles. While lying supine on a bench the athlete raises the dumbbells from the sides to an upward position. Like the pull-overs the lateral raises lying supply poor leverage, and only light weights can be used. To make the chest muscles do the work the arms are kept rigid. Yet the arms are slightly bent to protect the elbows from strain. When being lowered the dumbbells are brought only slightly below bench level.

The *rowing exercises* can be carried out from two basic positions—bending forward (photo series 29) or standing upright (photo series 30). In our illustrations the exercises are being done with a barbell. Dumbbells could be used just as well, but they would have to be very heavily loaded. The rowing exercises often involve considerable resistance, and this is the reason that a barbell tends to be more convenient.

In performing bent-over rowing, even though you are probably starting with light poundage, it is important to establish safe lifting habits early in the game. When lifting the barbell into the starting position for the rowing motion keep your head up and your back straight. A comfortable and stable position is assumed to counter the pull of the weight. The elbows are at your sides, and the barbell is pulled straight up. Carry out the rowing motion without getting any help from either trunk movement or your legs. Bent-over rowing develops the arms and the latissimus dorsi, the muscles in the upper back that draw the arms backward and downward and rotate them inward.

In upright rowing the trunk is erect and the legs stay straight. Hold your hands close together and keep your elbows as high as possible as you lift. The weight is pulled straight upward passing close to the body. Upright rowing not only develops the arms but is also excellent for the trapezius and deltoid muscles.

The *shoulder shrug* (photo series 31) offers a direct way of exercising the trapezius, the muscle that raises the shoulders. Rather heavy weights can be used with either a barbell or dumbbells. The arms are permitted to hang, and a rolling movement is carried out by the neck and shoulder muscles. The shoulders are brought through the largest possible circle. During the movement, lower your shoulders as far down as they will go, and then raise them as high as you can.

Side bending (photo series 32) strengthens the external oblique muscles, the muscles on the sides of the abdomen. Letting a dumbbell hang freely from one arm, bend sideways as far as possible. Then straighten up and bend to the other side. Avoid leaning either forward or backward. When you have finished the number of repetitions that you want, switch the weight to the other hand for an equal number of repetitions. The muscles developed by side bending serve to flex and rotate the trunk. Thus, they play a vital role in most sports.

Sit-ups (photo series 33), or trunk raises while lying on your back, give you a direct and effective way to strengthen your stomach wall (photo 34). Though many of the exercises already demonstrated affect the abdomen, direct attention to this area is desirable. It's likely that sit-ups are already familiar to you. As you make progress and achieve some preliminary conditioning, you can increase the resistance offered by the sit-ups by holding a barbell plate in back of your neck.

The *v-ups* (photo series 35) are a more advanced and difficult version of the sit-ups. The trunk and legs are raised together. It's not an easy exercise to perform. Practice is needed.

The *squat* (photo series 36), or knee-bend with a barbell across your shoulders, is the most valuable exercise for thigh and hip development and for developing over-all power. Wherever power is needed for an athletic event the squat is usually included in the training program. The squats affect various muscles of the body, but their greatest value lies in the effect they have on the quadriceps, the extensor muscles located in the front of the thigh (photo 37). This lifting and driving power is needed for nearly all sports activities.

This exercise more than any other has helped football players improve their drive, basketball players their spring, throwers their distance, and jumpers their height. As a matter of fact, the recent proliferation of high-jumpers able to clear seven feet can be credited to the use of squats.

Get very familiar with the squat, particularly with safety precautions, because you will be using fairly heavy weights. The barbell is placed on the shoulders either with the help of a reliable rack or with the assistance of training partners. Many gymnasiums have more advanced devices for controlling a heavy weight, and these devices offer increased safety features. The pressure exerted by the bar can be reduced by placing a towel over the shoulders or by wrapping the bar with a towel or with rubber tubing.

Be sure to take your time in getting the weight across your shoulders. Be sure that you have a balanced grip and feel comfortable and balanced. Keep your back straight. Most athletes use a board or other object to raise the heels and increase balance and comfort (photo series 38).

Many experienced coaches and trainers feel that it is best to abandon the full knee-bend in favor of the partial bend. They think that constant deep knee-bending causes both injuries and loss of running speed. Although this has not been proved, it would seem best to bend the legs only to that point where the thighs are parallel to the ground.

When you return the barbell to the rack, be just as careful as you were in getting it off.

Leg curls (photo 39) are used to strengthen the leg biceps and the hamstring tendons in the back of the thigh. "Iron boots" are worn to provide resistance. The athlete supports himself against a wall or other object. He stands on one leg and flexes the other. The curls can be performed either alternately or in alternate sets. That is, you can do a complete set of curls with one leg before exercising the other leg or go right leg, left leg, right, left, and so on.

Because so few other exercises involve the hamstrings (photo 40) to any large extent, these tendons are often neglected. Hence, the special importance of the leg curl.

Leg extensions. The "iron boots" permit the extensor muscles of the legs to be directly exercised. From a sitting position the legs are extended (photo series 41). The quadriceps (photo 42) carry out this exercise almost completely without the aid of other muscles. Thus, the leg extensions are highly valuable when the quadriceps muscles need special attention.

Dead lift (photo series 43). When correctly carried out the dead lift is a safe and highly valuable exercise. It develops the lower part of the body, including the lower back and the legs. The forearms become strengthened because a powerful grip is needed to hold the very heavy weights.

Correct execution of the dead lift is important. Take a comfortable position as close as you can get to the weight. Your shins should brush the bar.

Bend your legs. In gripping the bar one hand is placed palm down and the other palm up. As soon as you feel ready to lift, look up and straighten your back. Straighten your legs to start the lift, and as you stand up transfer some of the effort to your back, always remembering to keep your back straight. When you lower the weight to the floor, keep your head up and your back flat. After completing a set of repetitions, reverse your hands.

Heel-raise (photo series 44). Heavy weights are used. Hence, the procedure for taking the barbell off the rack and returning it to the rack is similar to that followed in the squat. The balls of the feet are placed on the board, and the heels are raised and lowered.

Heel-raises develop the calves of the legs, but it takes a lot of work to bring about significant changes in these muscles. Two points are important. First, heavy resistance is needed, so the weights must become progressively heavier. Second, there must be a full range of flexion. Raise your heels fully and lower them fully.

Reverse curl. Many of the basic exercises can be varied or changed somewhat. These variations have an effect upon the degree that different muscles are involved in the exercise. For example, in the normal curl there is great emphasis upon the biceps muscles.

However, if the hand grip is changed so that the palms are downward (photo series 45), the forearms play a more important part. Hence, the reverse curl is used when you want greater development of your forearms. In all other ways the reverse curl is done the same way as the ordinary curl.

Press behind the neck (photo series 46). The press can be started behind the neck with the weight resting on the back of the shoulders. In this variation a widely spaced grip is taken. As in the normal press the triceps play a large part in raising the weight, but the press behind the neck extends the exercise to increase the use of the deltoids, or muscles of the shoulders.

Hack lift (photo series 47). This lift gives you a somewhat different way of performing knee-bends with a barbell (photo series 49). Squat with your back toward the weight and grasp the bar. Keep your head up and your back straight. The lifting is done with your legs.

Like the squat the hack lift develops the extensors (the pushing muscles) of the thighs, but it affects them a little differently and thus is a useful variation. Also, handling a heavy weight strengthens the grip.

These then are some of the basic exercises. It is largely from these that you will select your programs. Study each exercise. The techniques are basically simple, but learn them well. Work with light weights until each exercise is familiar. Above all, observe all safety measures.

11. *Two-arms clean and press.* (*a*) A position close to the bar. Legs are bent. Ready to start the clean. (*b*) The clean is underway. Even though the weight is getting high, the legs are still driving. (*c*) The clean is completed, and the lifter is ready for the press. (*d*) The weight is overhead. The lift is completed.

11*a*

11*b*

12. *Two-arms snatch.* (*a*) The arms are more widely spaced than in the press. (*b*) The legs and back have gotten the weight underway. (*c*) The weight is pulled close to the body. The legs and back have finished pulling. The lifter is ready for the split. (*d*) A drop into the split position puts him under the weight. (*e*) Erect with the weight overhead.

11*c*

12*a*

11*d*

12*b*

12c

12d

12e

13. *Two-arms clean and jerk.* In (b) the weight is well on its way upward and the arms are just beginning to come into play. A squat (c) puts the lifter under the weight. By (e) the clean is finished, and he is ready for the jerk. The legs bend (f) in preparation for a drive. At (g) he has driven the weight overhead, splitting beneath it. Lift completed (h).

13a

13b

13c

13*d*

13*h*

13*e*

14. A thorough warm-up is an important part of every work-out.

13*f*

14*a*

13*g*

14*b*

→

14c

14d

14e

15. The press is one of the most widely used of the basic exercises. By (d) the weight has been brought into position for pressing. He is now ready for repetitions.

15a

15b

15c

15d

15e

15f

15g

15h

16. The clean must be carried out correctly. Legs and back play the major roles in getting the weight into position for the press.

16a

16b

16c

16d

17. The normal press emphasizes the triceps muscle.

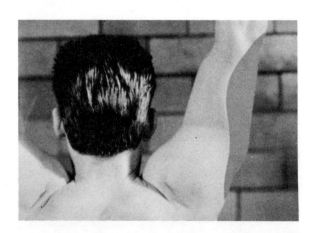

18. *Curl.* Body is erect. The elbows are kept close to the body. Flexion of the arms raises the weight.

18a

18b

18c

18d

18e

18f

19. *Bench press.* A sturdy bench is important, and a rack is useful. The barbell is raised from the chest to an upward position. With a narrow spacing of the hands the triceps muscles are most affected.

19a

19b

19c

19d

19e

19f

20. The deltoid (shoulder muscle) is divided into three parts—the front third, the middle third, and the back third. Its job is to raise the arms.

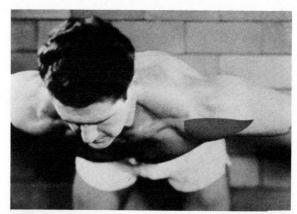

20a

20b

20c

21. *Lateral raises standing*. The dumbbells are raised sideways to a position directly overhead. The arms are bent only enough to take some of the strain off the elbows.

21*d*

21*a*

21*e*

21*b*

21*f*

21*c*

22. *Forward raises.* These can be carried out alternately. One arm is brought forward and up and then the other.

22d

22a

22e

22b

22f

22c

22g

22h

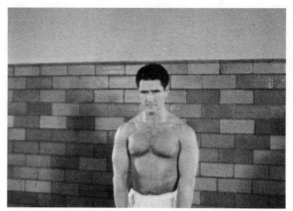

23a

22i

23b

23c

23. *Forward raises.* Both arms can be raised and lowered together.

23d

→

23e

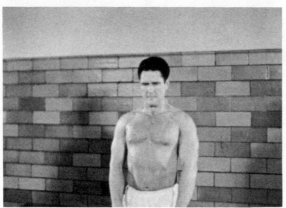

23f

24. *Lateral raises* can be performed from a bent-over position. From this same position backward raises can be carried out.

24a

24b

24c

24d

24e

25. *Straight-arm pull-over.* From a straight-up position the barbell is lowered back over the head to bench level. It is then brought back up. As the weight is lowered, inhale fully. Exhale fully as the weight rises.

25*d*

25*a*

25*e*

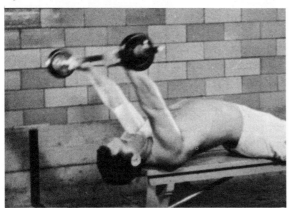

25*b*

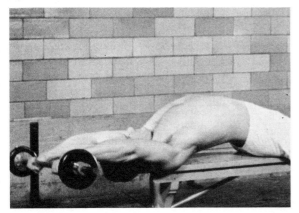

25*c*

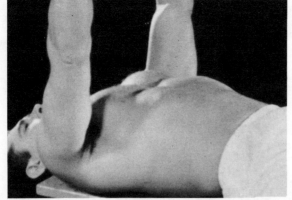

26a

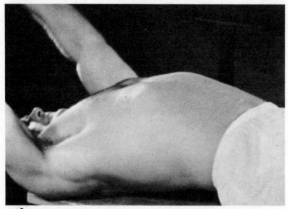

26b

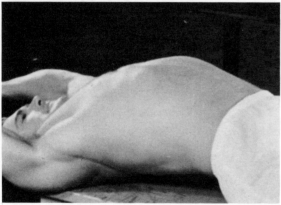

26c

26. Deep breathing pull-overs tend to increase the size of the rib cage.

27. *Lateral raises lying* or "flying exercises." The dumbbells are raised from the sides to an upward position. In carrying out repetitions the dumbbells are lowered only slightly below the level of the bench. The arms are slightly bent to protect the elbows from strain.

27a

27b

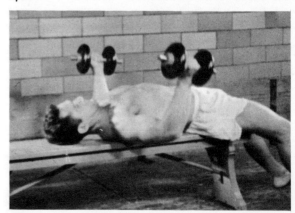

27c

27d

27e

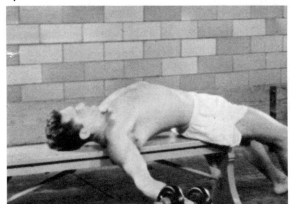

27f

28. "Flying exercises" are excellent for developing the chest muscles.

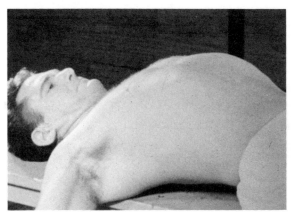

28a

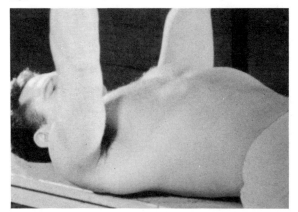

28b

29. *Bent-over rowing.* A wide grip is taken
(*a*) and vision is up. The legs are straightened
to pull the weight clear of the floor (*b*). The
rowing action brings the bar to the upper part
of the chest (*d*). The body should be in a
comfortable and stable position, but the arms
do all the lifting.

29*d*

29*a*

29*e*

29*b*

29*f*

29*c*

30. *Upright rowing.* In lifting the weight into position (*a* and *b*) the head is up and the back remains flat. Lifting is done with the legs. The hands are close together. After the body is erect the bar is pulled upward to shoulder level.

30*d*

30*a*

30*e*

30*b*

30*f*

30*c*

30*g*

31. *Shoulder shrug.* In (*a*) the arms hang at the side. Heavy dumbbells are used. The arms continue to hang and the shoulders roll through the largest possible circle. The shoulders are raised and lowered as far as they can go.

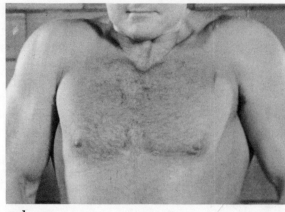

31*d*

31*a*

31*e*

31*b*

31*f*

31*c*

32. *Side bends.* With a dumbbell hanging downward and arm extended the athlete bends sideways as far as possible . . . then to the other side. Feet are close together. He avoids leaning either forward or backward. The dumbbell is switched to the other hand for an equal number of repetitions.

32d

32a

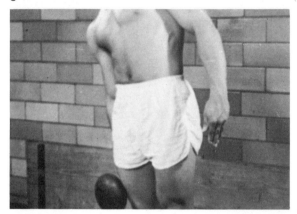

32e

32b

32f

32c

32g

32h

32l

32i

32j

33. *Sit-ups.* An old and familiar exercise but still an important one in building a strong stomach wall. Resistance can be increased by holding a plate in back of the neck.

33a

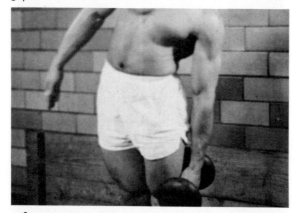

32k

33b

33*c*

33*g*

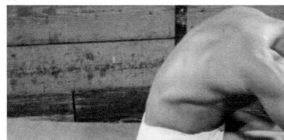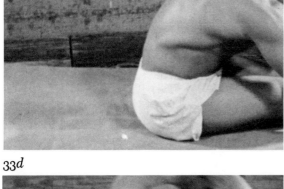

33*d*

33*h*

33*e*

34. The rectus abdominus flexes the trunk and is important to nearly all athletic activity.

33*f*

35. *V-ups.* The upper and lower parts of the body are raised together to form a "V." It takes practice to master this exercise, but it is worth it.

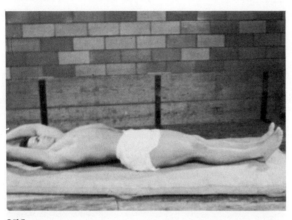

35*a*

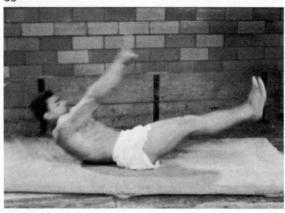

35*b*

35*c*

35*d*

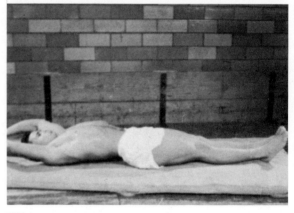

35*e*

36. *Squats* or *knee bends*. Preparing to take the barbell from the rack the athlete makes sure (*b*) that the weight will be well balanced on his shoulders. In (*c*) a straightening of the legs picks the barbell off the rack. He moves clear of the rack (*d*) and is ready to squat (*e*). Notice that head is always up and the trunk straight.

36*d*

36*a*

36*e*

36*b*

36*f*

36*c*

36*g*

→

36h

36i

38. Most athletes find that both balance and comfort are increased if a board or other object is used to raise the heels.

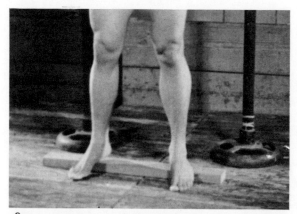

38a

38b

37. Squats develop the extensor muscles of the legs. Nearly all athletes need powerful thigh muscles.

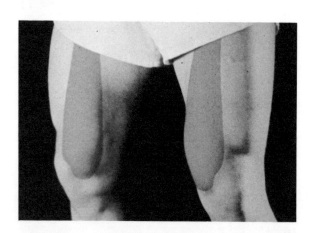

38c

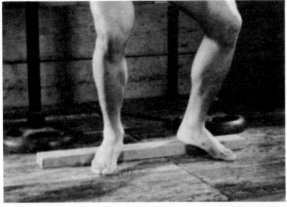

38d

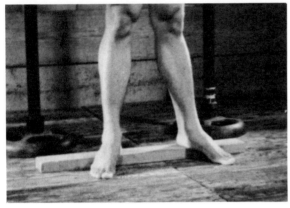

38e

39b

39c

39d

39. *Leg curls.* The athlete wears "iron boots," which are a kind of metal sandal that permits plates to be added in the manner of a dumbbell. Standing on one leg he flexes the other.

39a

39e

40. The average exercise program tends to neglect the hamstring tendons, located in the back of the thigh.

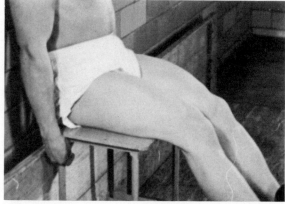

41b

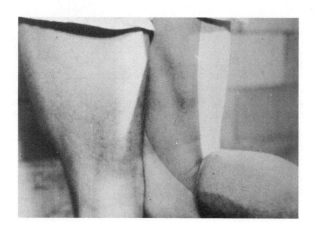

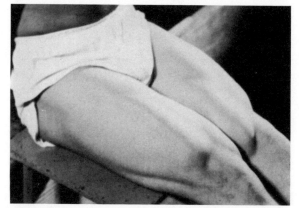

41c

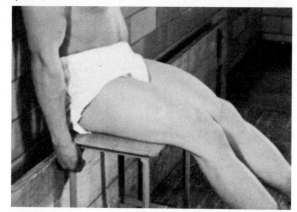

41d

41. *Leg extensions*. While sitting the legs are extended to raise the "iron boots." Both legs are being raised together, but the exercise can be carried out one leg at a time.

41a

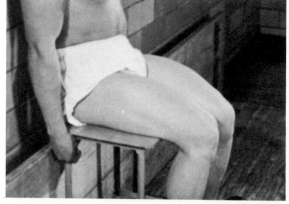

41e

42. Leg extensions are direct developers of the quadriceps.

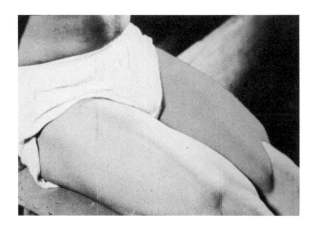

43. *Dead lift.* In (*a*) a position is carefully taken with the shins brushing the bar. The legs are bent. One hand is palm down and the other palm up. As he gets ready to lift (*b*), vision is up. A straightening of the legs starts the lift. By (*e*) the athlete is erect. In returning the weight to the floor the head remains up.

43*b*

43*c*

43*d*

43*a*

43*e*

→

43f

43g

43h

44. *Heel raise.* The weight is taken from the rack the same way as in the squat. The barbell is carefully centered on the shoulders and then lifted with the legs. The balls of the feet are placed on a board. The heels are lowered and raised fully.

44a

44b

44c

44d

44e

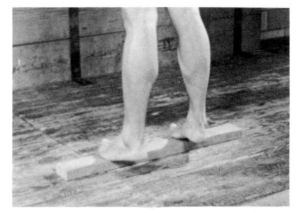

44g

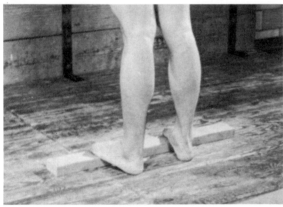

44f

44h

44i

45. *Reverse curl.* The hand grip is changed so that the palms are downward. In this way the forearms get more work. The movements of this exercise are the same as for the normal curl.

45*d*

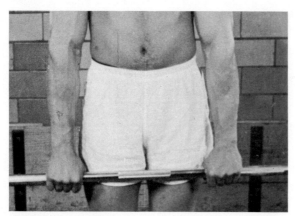

45*a*

45*e*

45*b*

46. *Press behind the neck.* The grip is wide. The press is started from behind the neck with the bar resting on the shoulders and lowered to the same position. In this variation of the press the shoulder muscles are strongly involved.

45*c*

46*a*

46b

46c

46d

46e

46f

47. *Hack lift.* In (*a*, *b*, and *c*) the athlete is taking position. Back is toward the weight. He squats as close as possible to the bar. By (*d*) he is ready to lift. Note that head is up and back is straight. The legs do the lifting (*e* and *f*). As the barbell is lowered (*g*), the head remains up and the back stays straight.

47a

47b

→

47c

47d

47e

47f

47g

Your Program

As soon as you get some confidence in your ability to carry out the basic exercises, you will want to set up your training program. Your program will, of course, be designed to make you better in the athletic event that you have chosen. At the present time establishing a program is not really a science. It is more of an art. It takes a lot of trial and error to discover what seems to be the best program for you. Even when you find one you will be changing it from time to time.

There is surely no single program that is best for all athletes in any one event. And perhaps no athlete has ever found the program that is absolutely best for him. Fine athletes are always experimenting in their search for more effective programs.

So don't be at all concerned that your first program will not be perfect. It is still going to do you a lot of good, especially if it is sensibly conceived. The important thing is to get started. You will need a starting program even though it is temporary.

If you are on a team get all of the help you can from your coach. He can take account of your age, condition, and other factors. Also, some members of your team may be able to pass along experience to you.

No matter how you acquire your first program, whether it is assigned by a coach, suggested by a teammate, or figured out by yourself, there are certain factors that will shape it. Exercises have to be selected. The numbers of repetitions and sets have to be determined, and you will have to decide on the frequency of work-out sessions. Let's talk a little about these.

Selection of exercises. In general, the way exercises are selected for a program is as follows. An event is analyzed to see which muscles are most important to good performance. Then exercises are selected that develop those particular muscles. This method is certainly a sound one and seems to work very well in practice. However, it is important to keep in mind that the match between the muscle needs of the event and the exercises is not as precise as most athletes and coaches seem to think.

In almost any athletic activity many muscles play a part. At any one moment some muscles play a bigger part than others. We may say that there is a gradient of muscle involvement. By that we mean that muscle *A* may be more involved than muscle *B*, which in turn may be more involved than *C*, and so on. To a lesser extent the same pattern holds true for most of the basic exercises.

In building a sensible weight-training program we will, of course, make an effort to select those exercises most appropriate to the athlete's event. But there is much more leeway than people think. You don't have to be too worried about a precise match between your event and the exercises selected. Besides, good performance in most activities requires all-round strength. The stronger you are the better you will perform.

Repetitions and sets. Weight-training programs are built around a framework of "reps" and sets. The word "reps" refers to the number of times that you perform an exercise without stopping. For example, if you press a weight over your head five times in a row you will have done five reps. If you stop and then do five more presses you have done two sets of five reps.

A program does not have to be completely cut and dried. You can change either the poundage or the number of reps or both. There are lots of ways of doing it. For example, in a program designed to develop great strength an athlete may, on some days, increase the poundage on each set to the point where he can only carry out one rep.

Starting weight. How much weight should you use when you first start? That will depend on your age, body weight, strength, and condition. And, of course, the exercise itself is important. In carrying out leg exercises you can for the most part handle more weight than in arm exercises. Also, some exercises, such as flying exercises and pull-overs, afford poor leverage, and only light weights can be used.

When you are first getting familiar with the exercises work with very light weights. For some exercises the bar alone might be enough for a start. You should not add much weight until you feel that you can perform the exercises correctly. It is especially important that you learn good safety habits.

56

Later on, as you become experienced in weight training, you will know almost instinctively the poundages to use and how to vary your routine. Also, you will probably have the chance to trade experiences and suggestions with other athletes training for your event. However, right now you have got to make a start. Let's assume that you have pretty well mastered the basic exercises and are ready to start using more weight.

We do not have enough experimental knowledge to be certain of the best way of getting started. But a number of plans seem to be highly successful. Here is one way to begin. Decide that you will do three sets of eight reps of a particular exercise. It will only take a little trial to find out the poundages that you can handle. If you cannot carry out the three sets of eight reps, obviously the weight is too heavy. If it is done too easily, it is too light. The correct amount of weight will make you feel that you have done some work, that the last few reps did not come too easily. The process of finding the correct starting poundages will not take long.

As you become stronger, you are going to find that doing the three sets of eight reps is easier. Keep the same amount of weight but increase the reps to nine. When that gets easier increase the reps to ten and so on until the reps get to twelve. At this point increase the amount of weight so that you can do only three sets of eight reps. Again, work your way up to three sets of twelve reps and again increase the amount of weight, going back to three sets of eight reps.

There is nothing extraordinary about this formula. It just seems to work well and is a good way to get started with most exercises. When you do squats and heel raises, however, you should start with more reps—probably twelve to fifteen. Also, with these leg exercises you will find that the increases in poundage can be greater.

Frequency of training. How many days each week should you weight train? First, that is going to depend on the time of year. You will lift more during your off-season than you will when your competitive season rolls around. Let's consider the off-season.

This is the time for your most intensive weight-training program. Important to muscle building is the idea that the fibers must be stimulated, allowed a period of rest, stimulated again, and so on. And, of course, all this must be done on a regular and systematic basis.

At present most authorities seem to think that a rest of one day between work-out sessions is about right. We cannot be sure that this is the best interval of rest, but it works well. You would then lift every other day during the off-season. You might weight train either Monday, Wednesday, and Friday or Tuesday, Thursday, and Saturday. Notice that at the beginning you are always off on Sunday. It may not always be that way.

The trend in most sports has been to find that we can work harder and more frequently than was previously thought. This may prove to be so in weight training. Hence, keep an eye on developments and be prepared to increase your work schedule if experience and research indicate that it should be done.

Even now, a number of fine athletes feel that they do best by weight training every day, but they emphasize different muscle groups on adjacent days. For example, one day they may select exercises that work the legs and the next day include exercises that stress upper-body development.

When you get into your competitive season you will probably lift less often. Some years ago, when weight training first became a standard routine for athletes, lifting was carried out only during the off-season. As soon as competition started, weight training was abandoned. But athletes began to find that they went into a "mid-season slump." They discovered that they could often get out of the slump by going back to weight training for one day each week. In some cases it grew to two days a week.

If it is at all possible, you ought to do at least some weight training during your competitive season. It will seldom be easy. For example, intensive football or basketball practice sessions will obviously reduce the amount of time and energy available for weight training.

An Example of Program Building

In this section let's take a look at a specific example of program building. Naturally, the particular contents of programs are going to vary according to any athlete's particular event. Yet it is useful to see the thinking that goes into building a program, because the thinking will be about the same regardless of the athletic event involved.

Suppose we follow the activities of a young high-school boy who has become a candidate for the shot-put. Let's see how he and his coach go about setting up a weight-training program.

The candidate has had some preliminary conditioning and has learned something about the technique of shot-putting. By this time it has been clearly established that he has apititude for the event that he has chosen (photo series 48). This is important, because it can save disappointment later on. If a candidate does not have aptitude for a particular event, it will be much more rewarding to find an activity more in line with his talents. The main function of the weight-training program is to bring out potential. A certain amount of it has to be there in the first place.

Without a weight-training program our candidate might still achieve fairly well. But if he is ambitious to approach his full potential and become a fine performer, a weight-training program is essential. All the best shot-putters in the world train with weights. Lifting may make a difference of ten or more feet in eventual performance.

Like most athletic activities the shot-put uses nearly all of the body's muscles. It is in itself a good form of exercise, but the event alone does not supply the progressive resistance needed for full development. In fact, as you get better and better at putting the shot, its exercise value becomes less and less. The same is true for nearly all athletic events.

A very young athlete's first program should be general. There are two related goals. First, all-round development is desirable. Second, the candidate should become well acquainted with all of the basic weight-training exercises.

Behind almost every fine athlete is a fine coach. If you can get the help of an instructor or experienced weight trainer, by all means do so. He can help you to learn the execution of the various exercises. Most important, he can help you to learn safe lifting habits, which will reduce the chance of injuries later on when heavier weights are used.

For example, in cleaning a weight (photo series 49) our candidate's coach teaches him to stand very close to the barbell. The beginner learns that it is essential to keep his head up and his back straight. He is taught that a straight back is important in carrying out almost any lift. He learns to take a position of balance and comfort over bent legs, that the legs start the lift.

The early training is general and continues with very little regard for the candidate's specific event. Light weights are used to help him get familiar with the exercises. Safety habits in lifting are constantly stressed.

Remember that our candidate is undergoing weight training primarily to become strong. He especially wants to strengthen the muscles most important to his event. Yet an important secondary process is going on. Good lifting habits are good athletic habits! He is learning balance, economy of movement, and the use of his legs.

It is only after a period of conditioning and background work that attention is concerned with exercises involving the event itself. Then a program can be worked out to emphasize the development of those muscles that play a major role in the candidate's chosen event.

In building a program for a particular event we have to keep in mind that in athletic activities nearly all muscles of the body are active. Muscles do not work in isolation, though a particular athletic event usually emphasizes certain muscles. These muscles become more important to performance than others. So we want these muscles to be well developed. Hence, in setting up our program we want a reasonably good match. The event and the exercises should both emphasize the same muscles.

As we watch the shot-put, it becomes clear that this event puts a great premium on strength and power. It is explosive in nature. For this reason we know that our candidate is going to have to build great strength. Eventually then, our candidate must progress to heavier lifting. He will point toward a program stressing heavy weights and few repetitions.

Now let's take a more detailed look at the candidate's event, the shot-put. Looking at photo 50 we can see that the legs play a big part in shot-put performance, as they do in most athletic events. They are the main source of power in driving the shot. We can be sure that our candidate is going to need leg exercises. And, of course, squats are going to be central to his program.

The technique of the squat is not difficult, but, because heavy weights will eventually be used, it must be learned well (photo series 51). Right now, the weight that our beginner is handling is relatively light, but he must learn habits that will prepare him for heavy weights. He is taught how to take the barbell from the rack. He must be sure that the weight is carefully balanced on his shoulders. Before he actually tries to lift the barbell from the rack, he must feel comfortable and his trunk must be erect. Lifting from the rack is done entirely by the legs. The trunk is kept erect during the squats. In returning the barbell to the rack the candidate is taught to observe the same precautions as in removing it.

An ambitious shot-putter will want to include leg curls in his program (photo series 52). Wearing iron boots and grasping a solid support, he carries out repetitions with each leg. Leg curls build up the hamstrings and the leg biceps, which are usually neglected.

Powerful calves add distance to the shot-put, so the heel raise (photo series 53) is added to the program. With the balls of the feet on a board the heels are moved through a full extension. They go all the way up and all the way down.

The most obvious feature of shot-putting is the violent action of the arm (photo series 54). The arm drives from a bent to a straight position. This means that the triceps muscle plays a major role in putting the shot. It is clear that the various presses are going to be important in developing the powerful arm thrust needed for good performance.

The standing press (photo series 55), sometimes called the military press when it is executed with the feet together and the body held very straight, is an excellent developer of the triceps muscles. It will become a permanent part of the candidate's routine. However, the candidate for the shot-put will also want to include other presses in his program. All of the presses develop the triceps muscles, but they also develop other muscles. The muscles most emphasized depend upon the position from which the press is made. The standing press strongly involves the shoulder muscles.

If the weight is pressed from a bench (photo series 56) the relative arm action is the same as in the standing press, but since the chest muscles add their strength to the lift, much heavier weights can be used. The wider the spacing of the hands the more active the chest muscles become.

An incline board presents another basic way in which the press can be performed. A special bench can be used or else a strong board can be placed against a solid support (photo series 57). This is a favorite exercise of the great shot-putters. Not only are the triceps muscles strongly affected but the shoulder muscles and the chest muscles also get a good work-out.

These are three of the basic pressing exercises. There are even more variations, such as dumbell presses, presses behind the neck, and so on. At any one time, the shot-put candidate will probably have two of the press variations included in his training program.

Returning to photo series 54 you can see that the extension of the arm is in coordination with strong action of the shoulder and chest muscles. These muscles then are obviously important to good performance. Dumbbell raises (photo 58) provide a very direct way of exercising the shoulder muscles. This direct approach is useful even though the deltoids are involved in standing and incline presses. Similarly, even though the chest muscles are developed by bench pressing, a direct approach to working the chest muscles should be included in the program. For this reason lateral raises lying (photo series 59) are added.

The shot-putter moves across the circle and lands in a position from which he can deliver a powerful blow (photo series 60). The trunk is poised to make a big contribution to performance. The ability of the trunk to respond and drive the shot is going to depend upon the strength of the stomach muscles, the side muscles, and the lower back muscles. The stronger these muscles become the farther the shot is going to go.

Sit-ups (photo series 61) and other abdominal exercises are used to strengthen the stomach wall. Powerful abdominal muscles are assets not only in the shot-put but in the performance of almost any athletic event. When the sit-ups become easy to do, they can be intensified by carrying them out on an incline with the feet higher than the head or by holding a weight behind the neck.

Side bends (photo series 62) are used to develop the external obliques, or side muscles. In this way the power of the trunk is increased. During side bending the feet are kept together to make the trunk do the work.

The dead lift (photo series 63) is included for its value in developing a strong lower back. It is a simple lift, but it must be carried out correctly. As in all heavy lifting, the head is up and the back remains flat. The legs begin the lift.

From time to time the candidate will change his program. He will use variations of some of the lifts. But you can see how his first program was put together. His event was analyzed to see which muscles are most important to performance. We know the muscles that are emphasized by each of the basic weight-training exercises. We then tried for a reasonable match. The match is always approximate because muscles do not act in isolation. And, of course, in building the program an important over-all point was kept in mind: An athlete, especially a young one, should build all-round strength.

The resistance supplied by the weights must be progressive. In each exercise weight must be added as the present weights become easier to handle (photo series 64). The idea of progressive resistance is that the muscles grow stronger by gradually becoming used to greater and greater loads.

Running should always be a part of any training program. It is important in developing your circulatory system. If your own event does not involve running, it is especially important that you run regularly in order to develop endurance. The heavier your lifting program the more important running becomes as a health measure.

Never forget your event or sport. Work at it and master it. Weight training produces such remarkable results and has such a fascination in itself that some athletes forget why they started it. Remember that your basic reason for weight training is to perform well in your chosen event.

48. The candidate shows aptitude for his event but needs a weight-training program to bring out his potential.

48d

48a

48e

48b

48f

48c

49. An athlete is lucky if he can get the guidance of an experienced instructor. In cleaning the athlete is taught to get very close to the bar. He learns to keep his head up and his back flat. Safety measures should become habitual.

49*d*

49*a*

49*e*

49*b*

50. The legs play a big part in shot-put performance. The weight-training program will have to include squats and other leg exercises.

49*c*

51. The candidate is carefully instructed in the squat, since he will be handling heavy weights in the future. Safety measures are emphasized. He is taught to keep his head up, his back flat, and to do the work with his legs.

51d

51a

51e

51b

51f

51c

51g

51h

51i

51j

51k

52. Leg curls build up the hamstrings and flexors of the legs.

52a

52b

52c

53. In carrying out the heel raise the weight is taken from the rack in the same way as for squats. To help the calves develop further the weight eventually has to be heavy and there must be full flexion. Compare (*d*) with (*e*).

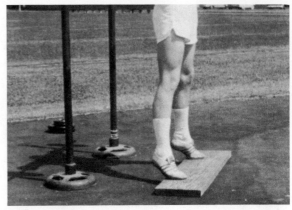
53*d*

53*a*

53*e*

53*b*

54. In putting the shot the movement of the arm is extension. The shot is pushed by driving the arm from a flexed position to an extended one. This means that the triceps muscles are important, and presses are going to be needed.

53*c*

54*a*

54b

54c

55. Where strong triceps are needed, the "military" press becomes a standard part of the training program.

55a

55b

55c

56. The bench press develops the triceps and extends the exercise to involve the chest muscles. Because the last rep is sometimes all-out, it is good to have help in returning the barbell to the rack.

56*a*

56*b*

56*c*

57*a*

57*b*

57*c*

57. The incline press is a favorite exercise of fine shot-putters. It works the triceps, the shoulder muscles, and the chest muscles.

58. The shot-put requires powerful shoulder muscles. Deltoid raises provide a direct approach to strengthening the shoulders.

59c

59. The chest muscles are involved in many exercises, but if they need direct attention nothing is better than "flying exercises."

59a

60. A powerful blow of the trunk is needed for good shot-put performance. Notice the full sweep of the trunk from (a) to (d). Exercises will be included that develop the stomach muscles, the side muscles, and the lower back muscles.

59b

60a

→

6o*b*

6o*c*

6o*d*

61. Strong abdominal muscles are needed not only in the shot-put but in nearly all sports.

61*a*

61*b*

61*c*

62. It takes strong external obliques (side muscles) to make a strong trunk. Side bends are excellent developers of these muscles.

63*a*

62*a*

63*b*

62*b*

63*c*

63. The lower part of the back is developed by the dead lift. Heavy weights will eventually be used, and for this reason safety measures are important. Note in (*c*) that before the actual lift is made the head goes up and the back flattens out.

63*d*

➜

63e

63f

64. Weight is added. Resistance should be progressive.

64a

64b

64c

Selecting Key Exercises

In the preceding section we examined the building of a program for a specific athletic event. Two major points were brought out. First, the athlete should develop all-round strength. The entire body is involved in most athletic activities. So the stronger you are, the better you will perform. It follows then that athletes with very different specialties will perform many exercises in common. Second, particular events can put a premium on certain muscles. Thus, in building a program these muscles should get special attention through the selection of appropriate weight-training exercises. In summary, there are two important aspects to a weight-training program. You want all-round strength, and at the same time you want to give special attention to those muscles that play a big part in your event.

If you analyze an event you can usually spot the muscles that are most important to it. Besides, for most athletic events a considerable body of knowledge has been accumulated by coaches and experienced athletes.

Suppose we take a look at a few more athletic activities. We are assuming that each athlete will have an all-round program. Our interest now is to see what exercises will be of special importance.

Discus. As we watch the discus throw (photo series 66), it becomes clear that the legs play an enormous role in performance. An effective turn requires strong legs. Also, the legs must contribute to the final drive. It is easy to see why the discus is often called a "leg event."

The discus thrower gives knee-bends a permanent and prominent place in his work-out schedule. Often partial squats are performed with very heavy weights. The knee-bends are sometimes deeper but never so deep as to jeopardize the leg speed so necessary to fine discus performance.

Every experienced coach knows that a strong arm alone will certainly not guarantee achievement in the dicus throw, but powerful arms are necessary. The contribution of the arm is obvious.

Both powerful biceps and forearms are needed. Curls (photo 67) are indicated. An athlete who is mature and in good condition can work with heavy weights and few repetitions. Because the discus throw is a power event, the athlete must be prepared to lift heavy weights.

The discus throw is a twisting, or centrifugal, event. It is the function of the pectorals to draw the arms inward. As we would expect, these chest muscles play a vital part in delivering power to the discus. Therefore the pectorals are going to get special attention both by lateral raises lying (photo series 68) and bench presses (photo 69).

High Jump. As do so many other athletic events, the high jump calls for a program of all-round development. Of course, strong legs are essential, but it has been found that great performance also requires a generally strong body.

Today, the typical weight-training program for a fine high jumper almost looks as if it were designed for a weight thrower. Jumpers train to strengthen all parts of their bodies. Many of them even practice the international lifts (photo series 70) in order to develop explosive power.

The high jumper of a generation ago did little more than stretch and jog. He was even afraid to jump too much. But now not only does he lift but he works with heavy weights. As we look at it now, this development seems natural enough because the high jump is basically a power event.

Photo series 71 tells the main story. Assuming that the jumper's basic technique is sound, we see that his ability to get height is going to depend largely on the power with which he can extend his take-off leg. The greater the explosion, the higher he goes. Hence, even though he has a weight-training program designed to give him all-round development, a great part of his attention is going to be directed toward developing the extensor muscles of his legs. Squats (photo 72), and heavy ones, are going to be a steady and large portion of his training routine. For variation he may turn to the leg-pressing machine, a heavy steel frame that holds the weight in position while the lifter presses it upward. This exercise works the same muscles as do the squats, but with a slightly different emphasis.

Javelin. A strong throwing arm is important to javelin performance, but it is not enough. Excellent coordination and general muscular development are needed. Strong legs (photo series 73) are as essential as a strong arm. Powerful legs are necessary for a fast and controlled approach, and they are equally important in delivering an explosive blow to the javelin. Again, squats are central to the program. By now we can generalize and say that squats are needed in any athletic event in which power against the ground is needed.

As the thrower prepares to deliver the javelin (photo series 74), observe the powerful lift and forward movement of the trunk. Since a strong trunk is essential to good performance, the athlete's schedule includes various midsection exercises (photo series 75).

The javelin is thrown with a pulling action (photo series 76). We see that the implement is kept in the vertical plane and pulled overhead in a large arc. The straight arm pull-overs (photo series 77) are highly valuable here in that they develop the pulling muscles located in the shoulder and chest. The French curl (photo series 78) is a variation of the pull-over that closely resembles the javelin pull.

As we consider the various athletic events, a pattern begins to emerge. Nearly all the muscles of the body play a part in most athletic activities. All-round development is needed, and for this reason a weight-training program always contains a good number of the basic exercises. These will be varied from time to time. The athlete must have a generally strong body, but specific events put a premium on certain muscles. Good performance depends upon these muscles having special strength. An analysis of an event indicates what the important muscles are. Key exercises are selected, and these remain central to the training program.

65. Record keeping is important. The athlete records the date, exercises used, amount of weight, and the numbers of repetitions and sets.

66*b*

66*c*

66*d*

66. Powerful legs are needed for fine discus performance.

66*a*

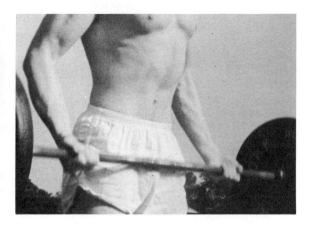

67. Clearly the discus thrower needs powerful arms. Both the biceps and triceps must be strong. Heavy curls are indicated.

68. The chest muscles supply much of the pull that whips the discus. "Flying exercises" give these muscles direct attention.

68a

68b

68c

68d

69. Widely spaced hands makes the bench press an excellent developer of the chest muscles.

70. Fine high jumpers often practice the international lifts for all-round development.

71a

70a

71b

70b

71c

71. A powerful extension of the jumping leg lifts the jumper. The stronger his legs the higher he goes.

70c

72. Squats will always be a big part of the jumper's program.

73. The javelin thrower's legs are as essential to performance as his arms.

73*a*

73*b*

74. A strong trunk helps drive the javelin.

74*a*

74*b*

74*c*

75. The midsection gets direct attention. A plate is held behind the neck to increase resistance.

76a

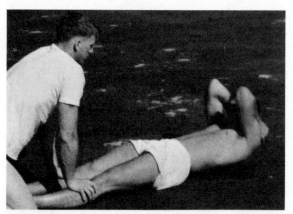

75a

76b

75b

76c

76. The javelin is pulled.

75c

77. Since the basic throwing action of the javelin is a pull, pull-overs become a part of the program.

78a

77a

78b

77b

78c

78. The French curl simulates the arm action of javelin throwing.

77c

Conclusion

This book will have served its purpose if you now know a little more about weight training. We hope that you are now quite convinced that weight training can make you a better athlete.

The American athlete always works better and with more enthusiasm if he understands the "why" of what he is doing. He does not like to work blindly or on just anyone's say so. Hence, it is useful for you to know the basic ways that muscles work and the astonishing way they respond to progressive resistance.

The effects of weight training on athletic performance have been so remarkable that this valuable method sometimes creates the impression of magic. We have tried to remove the magic and mystery. We have tried to show that building your program is mostly a matter of observation and common sense.

We trust that you have not been bored by the many references to safety and safe lifting habits. We hope not, because here is one more reminder. Develop safe lifting habits.

Profit as much as you can from your contacts with coaches and experienced athletes. They can certainly help you. But finally, it is all up to you. Your achievement lies in your own hands.

NOTES

NOTES

NOTES

ALSO AVAILABLE FROM PENGUIN BY DR. FRANK RYAN

Gymnastics for Girls

The most exciting event in the past Olympic games, women's gymnastics, has come into its own as one of the great sports of our time. It is also a breathtakingly beautiful sport, in which each competitor must demonstrate her skills in four unique and demanding categories: floor exercise, balance beam, uneven parallel bars, and the vault. In these pages, Dr. Frank Ryan tells you all you need to know about the fundamentals of gymnastics, about individual tumbling and dance skills, about control and precision, about the split-second timing of work on the uneven parallel bars, about the techniques of aggressive performance on the vault, and much more. The author also offers you invaluable advice on the development of combinations that will enable the gymnast to devise her own routines. Illustrated with dozens of step-by-step photographs, this is the most comprehensive guide available for today's young student—and tomorrow's champion.

Swimming Skills: Freestyle, Butterfly, Backstroke, Breaststroke

Previously published as four volumes, and now available for the first time in a comprehensive volume, *Swimming Skills* provides instruction and advice for proper training and physical mechanics that will benefit swimmers at every level of ability. Concerned with championship technique, and based on teaching films made with Phil Moriarty, Yale University's varsity swimming coach, this volume contains illustrations and actual full action sequences of the four basic swimming styles discussed. This volume serves as an invaluable guide to these four basic swimming strokes and will prove to be an important addition to your sports library.